Wilkins Surname

Ireland: 1600s to 1900s

From Ireland Church Records of Baptism, Marriage and Death

Comprised of Roman Catholic and Church of Ireland Records

From Counties Carlow, Cork, Kerry and Dublin City

Compiled by **Donovan Hurst**

February 26, 2013

ISBN: 1939958105
ISBN-13: 978-1-939958-10-5

Dedication

This work is dedicated to all of those that came before us and shaped our lives to make us the people that we are today.

Table of Contents

Introduction

This is a compilation of individuals who have the surname of Wilkins that lived in the country of Ireland from the 1600s to the 1900s. I have placed each entry into one of four categories: Families, Individual Births/Baptisms, Individual Burials, and Individual Marriages. If a marriage entry primarily concerns an Individual Wilkins whom is female, then I have placed that entry under the category of Individual Marriages. If a marriage entry primarily concerns an Individual Wilkins whom is male, then I have placed that entry under the category of Families. Images of many of these listings are available at http://churchrecords.irishgenealogy.ie/churchrecords/.

To help guide the reader of this work, the format of this book is as follows:

- Main Family Entry (Husband and Wife) (Father and Mother)

  o Child of Main Family Entry, including Spouse(s) when available

    ▪ Grandchild of Main Family Entry, including Spouse(s) when available

      • Great-Grandchild of Main Family Entry, including Spouse(s) when available

(**Bolded Text**) following any entry includes any additional information such as Residence(s), Occupation(s), Signature(s), etc. when available.

Hurst

Some of the fonts used in this work symbolizes Celtic writing. The traditional letters, numbers, and punctuation marks and their Celtic counterparts are as follows:

Traditional Letters (Uppercase & Lowercase)

A a B b C c D d E f G g H h I i J j K k L l M m N n O o P p Q q R r S s T t U u V v W w X x Y y Z z

Celtic Letters (Uppercase & Lowercase)

A a B b C c D ð E e F f G g H h I i J j K k L l M m

N n O o P p Q q R r S s T t U u V v W w X x Y y Z z

Traditional Numbers

1 2 3 4 5 6 7 8 9 10

Celtic Numbers

1 2 3 4 5 6 7 8 9 10

Traditional Punctuation

. , : ' " & - ( )

Celtic Punctuation

. , : ' " & - ( )

Parish Churches

Carlow (Church of Ireland)

Carlow Parish.

Cork & Ross (Roman Catholic or RC)

Cork - South Parish and Cork - SS. Peter & Paul Parish.

Dublin (Church of Ireland)

Arbour Hill Barracks Parish, Beggar's Bush Barracks Parish, Chapelizod Parish, Clondalkin Parish, Glasnevin Parish, Kilmainham Parish, Leeson Park Parish, Molyneux Chapel Parish, Portobello Barracks Parish, Rathmines Parish, Rotunda Chapel Parish, St. Andrew Parish, St. Anne Parish, St. Audoen Parish, St. Bride Parish, St. Catherine Parish, St. George Parish, St. James Parish, St. John Parish, St. Luke Parish, St. Mark Parish, St. Mary Parish, St. Mathew Parish, St. Michan Parish, St. Nicholas Within Parish, St. Nicholas Without Parish, St. Paul Parish, St. Peter Parish, St. Stephen Parish, St. Thomas Parish, and St. Werburgh Parish.

Dublin (Roman Catholic or RC)

Lucan Parish, Rathmines Parish, St. Agatha Parish, St. Andrew Parish, St. Catherine Parish, St. James Parish, St. Mary, Pro Cathedral Parish, St. Michan Parish, and St. Nicholas Parish.

Kerry (Church of Ireland)

Tralee Parish.

Kerry (Roman Catholic or RC)

Tralee Parish.

Families

- Andrew Wilkins & Unknown

  o Catherine Wilkins & George Kearns (K e a r n s) – 30 Sep 1867 (Marriage, **St. Werburgh Parish**)

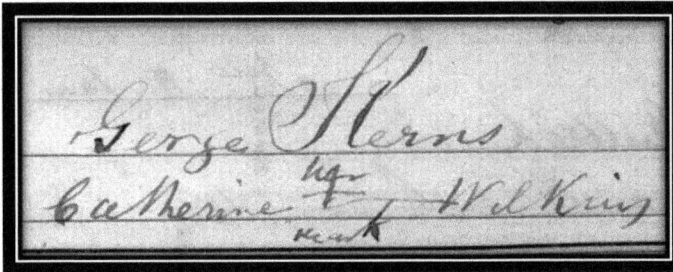

Signatures:

Catherine Wilkins (daughter):

   Residence - 42 Essex Street - September 30, 1867

George Kearns, son of Michael Kearns (son-in-law):

   Residence - 42 Essex Street - September 30, 1867

   Occupation - Shoemaker - September 30, 1867

Michael Kearns (father):

   Occupation - Laborer

Andrew Wilkins (father):

   Occupation - Cooper

Hurst

Wedding Witnesses:

John Barrett & Eleanor Barrett

Signatures:

- Charles Wilkins & Jane Robinson – 29 Jun 1841 (Marriage, **St. George Parish**)

Signatures:

- ○ Elizabeth Catherine Wilkins – b. 25 Mar 1843, bapt. 6 Apr 1843 (Baptism, **St. George Parish**)

Charles Wilkins (father):

Residence - Abbey Street, St. Mary Parish, Dublin - June 29, 1841

No. 40 Summer Street - April 6, 1843

Occupation - Solicitor - June 29, 1841

April 6, 1843

Jane Robinson (mother):

Residence - St. George Parish - June 29, 1841

Wilkins Surname Ireland: 1600s to 1900s

Wedding Witnesses:

Hercules Robinson, Thomas Bligh St. George, & James C. Coltingham

Signatures:

- Charles James Wilkins & Julia Hudson – 10 Jan 1818 (Marriage, **St. Peter Parish**)

Charles James Wilkins (husband):

   Residence - St. Anne Parish - January 10, 1818

Wedding Witnesses:

James Cook & G. Williams

- Edward Wilkins & Unknown

   o   Thomas Wilkins & Elizabeth Gavan – 20 Jul 1890 (Marriage, **St. Thomas Parish**)

Signatures:

Thomas Wilkins (son):

   Residence - Aldboro House Barracks - July 20, 1890

   Occupation - Corporal A S C - July 20, 1890

Hurst

Elizabeth Gavan, daughter of Michael Gavan (daughter-in-law):

Residence - 38 James Street - July 20, 1890

Michael Gavan (father):

Occupation - Butter Factor

Edward Wilkins (father):

Occupation - Groom

Wedding Witnesses:

Charles Swann & Elizabeth Ryan

Signatures:

- Francis Wilkins & Mary Unknown
  - Francis Wilkins – bapt. 15 Oct 1777 (Baptism, **St. Werburgh Parish**)

Francis Wilkins (father):

Residence - New Row - October 15, 1777

- Frederick Wilkins & Elizabeth Wilkins
  - Mary Wilkins – bapt. 18 Jan 1841 (Baptism, **Cork - SS Peter & Paul Parish (RC)**)

Wilkins Surname Ireland: 1600s to 1900s

- George Wilkins & Elizabeth Wilkins, bur. 19 Mar 1713 (Burial, **Carlow Parish**)

- George Wilkins, bur. 19 Jul 1798 (Burial, **St. Nicholas Without Parish**) & Mary Roche – 24 Dec 1773 (Marriage, **St. Andrew Parish**)

  o Martha Wilkins – bapt. 22 Aug 1779 (Baptism, **St. Nicholas Without Parish**)

  o William Wilkins – bapt. 27 Jun 1784 (Baptism, **St. Nicholas Without Parish**)

  o Mary Anne Wilkins – b. 10 Jan 1792, bapt. 27 Jan 1792 (Baptism, **St. Nicholas Without Parish**)

  o William Wilkins – b. 2 Nov 1795, bapt. 8 Nov 1795 (Baptism, **St. Nicholas Without Parish**)

  o Arabella Wilkins – bapt. 13 Jul 1798 (Baptism, **St. Nicholas Without Parish**)

George Wilkins (father):

Residence - Patrick Street - August 22, 1779

June 27, 1784

January 27, 1792

November 8, 1795

July 13, 1798

before July 19, 1798

- George Wilkins & Unknown

  o James Wilkins & Anne Jane Russell – 3 Oct 1877 (Marriage, **St. Peter Parish**)

Signatures:

Hurst

James Wilkins (son):

    Residence - 44 Scotch Street, Armagh - October 3, 1877

    Occupation - Jeweler - October 3, 1877

Anne Jane Russell, daughter of John Russell (daughter-in-law):

    Residence - 28 Kenilworth Square, Rathmines - October 3, 1877

John Russell (father):

    Occupation - Merchant

George Wilkins (father):

    Occupation - Farmer

Wedding Witnesses:

Richard Wilkins & Thomas Warshop

Signatures:

- George Eugene Cameron Wilkins & Jane Dickson
  - Henry Cornwall Christopher Wilkins – b. 31 Dec 1875, bapt. 12 Jan 1876 (Baptism, St. Agatha Parish (RC))

Wilkins Surname Ireland: 1600s to 1900s

George Eugene Cameron Wilkins (father):

    Residence - 10 William Street - January 12, 1876

- Gulielmo Wilkins & Mary Harrington

  - Margaret Wilkins – bapt. 31 Jul 1814 (Baptism, **St. Michan Parish (RC)**)

- Gulielmo Wilkins & Mary Unknown

  - Gulielmo Wilkins & Mary McDonnell – 1 Feb 1864 (Marriage, **St. Agatha Parish (RC)**)

    - Mary Anne Wilkins – b. 15 Feb 1865, bapt. 20 Feb 1865 (Baptism, **St. Mary, Pro Cathedral Parish (RC)**)

Gulielmo Wilkins (son):

    Residence - 4 Arran Street - February 1, 1864

        6 Lower Rutland Street - February 20, 1865

Mary McDonnell, daughter of John McDonnell & Anne Unknown (daughter-in-law):

    Residence - 2 Clonliffe - February 1, 1864

Wedding Witnesses:

Peter Carey & Elizabeth Murphy

- Henry Wilkins & Bridget Unknown

  - Thomas Henry Wilkins – bapt. 1838 (Baptism, **St. Andrew Parish (RC)**)

- Henry Wilkins & Jane McClean

  - George Angus Cameron Wilkins – bapt. 25 Sep 1872 (Baptism, **St. Mary, Pro Cathedral Parish (RC)**)

Hurst

Henry Wilkins (father):

Residence - Aldboro Barracks - September 25, 1872

- Henry Wilkins & Jane Unknown
  - George Wilkins & Jane McDonald – 8 Feb 1875 (Marriage, **St. Mary, Pro Cathedral Parish (RC)**)

George Wilkins (son):

Residence - Aldborough House - February 8, 1875

Jane McDonald, daughter of John McDonald & Hannah Dixon (daughter-in-law):

Residence - 3 Hutton's Lane - February 8, 1875

Wedding Witnesses:

James Dixon & Mary Dixon

- Henry Wilkins & Mary Hardinge
  - Frederick Henry Wilkins – bapt. 15 May 1840 (Baptism, **St. Nicholas Parish (RC)**)
- Henry Wilkins & Mary Oldham – 20 Jul 1805 (Marriage, **St. Paul Parish**)
- Henry Wilkins & Mary Wilkins
  - John Wilkins – b. 1 May 1842, bapt. 5 Jun 1842 (Baptism, **St. Catherine Parish**), bapt. 12 Jun 1842 (Baptism, **St. Catherine Parish (RC)**), bur. 11 Sep 1842 (Burial, **St. Catherine Parish**)

John Wilkins (son):

Residence - Summer Street - before September 11, 1842

Age at Death - 2 months

Wilkins Surname Ireland: 1600s to 1900s

Henry Wilkins (father):

Residence - 6 Summer Street - June 5, 1842

Occupation - Tailor - June 5, 1842

- James Wilkins & Martha Unknown
  - John Wilkins – bapt. 22 Mar 1785 (Baptism, **St. Nicholas Without Parish**)
  - Joseph Wilkins – b. 3 Jun 1786, bapt. 7 Jun 1786 (Baptism, **St. Nicholas Without Parish**)
  - Arabella Wilkins – b. 1788, bapt. 1788 (Baptism, **Clondalkin Parish**)
  - Jeremiah Wilkins – b. 19 Nov 1789, bapt. 22 Nov 1789 (Baptism, **St. Nicholas Without Parish**)
  - William Wilkins – b. 1790, bapt. 1790 (Baptism, **Clondalkin Parish**)

James Wilkins (father):

Residence - Patrick Street - March 22, 1785

June 7, 1786

Grange - 1788

1790

Francis Street - November 22, 1789

- James Wilkins & Mary Sheridan – 12 Feb 1844 (Marriage, **St. Peter Parish**)

James Wilkins (husband):

Residence - Leinster Terrace - February 12, 1844

Mary Sheridan (wife):

Residence - Leinster Terrace - February 12, 1844

Wedding Witnesses:

Margaret Sexton & Thomas Sheldon

- James Wilkins & Mary Unknown

  o Anne Jane Wilkins – b. 18 Mar 1836, bapt. 3 Apr 1836 (Baptism, **St. Peter Parish**)

James Wilkins (father):

Residence - 18 South King Street - April 3, 1836

- James Wilkins & Unknown

  o Ellen Wilkins & Thomas Pakenham – 24 May 1882 (Marriage, **Rathmines Parish**)

Signatures:

Ellen Wilkins (daughter):

Residence - 135 Leinster Road - May 24, 1882

Occupation - Domestic Servant - May 24, 1882

Thomas Pakenham, son of William Pakenham (son-in-law):

Residence - 6 Garden Terrace Upper Clanbrassil Street - May 24, 1882

Occupation - Of Her Majesty's Post Office - May 24, 1882

Relationship Status at Marriage - widow

Wilkins Surname Ireland: 1600s to 1900s

William Pakenham (father):

    Occupation - Game Keeper

James Wilkins (father):

    Occupation - Farmer

Wedding Witnesses:

Thomas Grant & Mary Grant

Signatures:

- James Wilkins & Unknown
  - Martha Wilkins & William Lynham – 27 Apr 1897 (Marriage, **St. Anne Parish**)

Signatures:

Martha Wilkins (daughter):

    Residence - 13 South Frederick Street, Dublin - April 27, 1897

Hurst

William Lynham, son of John Lynham (son-in-law):

    Residence - Geashill, King's County - April 27, 1897

    Occupation - Church Sexton - April 27, 1897

John Lynam (father):

    Occupation - Church Sexton

James Wilkins (father):

    Occupation - Farmer

Wedding Witnesses:

Alfred Warren & Elizabeth Jane Wilkins

Signatures:

- John Wilkins & Anne Wilkins

  - Lucy Wilkins – bapt. 5 Feb 1806 (Baptism, **St. Mary Parish**)

  - Margaret Wilkins – bapt. 5 Feb 1806 (Baptism, **St. Mary Parish**)

  - Anne Wilkins – bapt. 6 Sep 1807 (Baptism, **St. Mary Parish**)

  - Henry Wilkins – bapt. 23 Aug 1813 (Baptism, **St. Mary Parish**)

  - Harriet Wilkins – bapt. 10 Jul 1818 (Baptism, **St. Mary Parish**)

Wilkins Surname Ireland: 1600s to 1900s

- John Wilkins & Catherine Wilkins

  o Alfred Thomas Wilkins – b. 18 May 1879, bapt. 13 Jul 1879 (Baptism, **Beggar's Bush Barracks Parish**)

John Wilkins (father):

Residence - Beggar's Bush Barracks - July 13, 1879

Occupation - Private, 77th Regiment, D. C. O. [De-commissioned Officer] **- July 13, 1879**

- John Wilkins & Elizabeth Wilkins

  o Robert Wilkins – bapt. 24 Oct 1737 (Baptism, **St. Luke Parish**)

- John Wilkins & Ellen Reardon

  o Helen Honor Wilkins – bapt. 2 Apr 1850 (Baptism, **Cork - South Parish (RC)**)

- John Wilkins & Mabel Wilkins

  o John Wilkins – bur. 18 Dec 1686 (Burial, **St. Michan Parish**)

John Wilkins (father):

Occupation - Laborer - December 18, 1686

- John Wilkins & Margaret Farrell – Apr 1757 (Marriage, **St. Werburgh Parish**)

  o Edward Wilkins – bapt. 22 Jul 1758 (Baptism, **St. Werburgh Parish**)

  o Samuel Wilkins – bapt. 21 Oct 1761 (Baptism, **St. Werburgh Parish**)

John Wilkins (father):

Residence - Crane Lane - July 22, 1758

October 21, 1761

- John Wilkins & Mary Unknown Sheppard – 28 Feb 1749 (Marriage, **St. Bride Parish**)

John Wilkins (husband):

  Occupation - Glazier - February 28, 1749

Mary Unknown Sheppard (wife):

  Relationship Status at Marriage - widow

- John Wilkins & Sarah Miles Wilkins
  - Charles Bertie Wilkins – b. 6 Jun 1867, bapt. 24 Jun 1868 (Baptism, **Portobello Barracks Parish**)

John Wilkins (father):

  Residence - Portobello Barracks - June 24, 1868

  Occupation - Queen's or 2nd Master Sergeant, Royal Horse Artillery - June 24, 1868

- John Wilkins & Susan Wilkins
  - George Lewis Wilkins – b. 27 Aug 1813, bapt. 5 Sep 1813 (Baptism, **St. Luke Parish**)
- John Wilkins & Unknown
  - Anne Wilkins & Richard Johnson – 17 Sep 1849 (Marriage, **St. Thomas Parish**)

Signatures:

Anne Wilkins (daughter):

  Residence - 17 Werburgh Place - September 17, 1849

Wilkins Surname Ireland: 1600s to 1900s

Richard Johnson, son of Charles Johnson (son-in-law):

Residence - 17 Werburgh Place - September 17, 1849

Occupation - Paper Stainer - September 17, 1849

Relationship Status at Marriage - widow

Charles Johnson (father):

Occupation - Paper Stainer

John Wilkins (father):

Occupation - Tailor

Wedding Witnesses:

Gerland Mahony & Daniel Mahony

Signatures:

o   Harriet Wilkins & William Armstrong (A r m s t r o n g) – 26 Dec 1851 (Marriage, **St. Peter Parish**)

Signatures:

Harriet Wilkins (daughter):

> Residence - 18 Harold's Cross - December 26, 1851

William Armstrong, son of James Armstrong (son-in-law):

> Residence - 31 Upper Baggot Street - December 26, 1851

> Occupation - Shop Keeper - December 26, 1851

James Armstrong (father):

> Occupation - Gentleman

John Wilkins (father):

> Occupation - Tailor

Wedding Witnesses:

John Wilkins & James Malone

Signatures:

- John Wilkins & Unknown

  o Joseph Lewis Wilkins & Elizabeth Matthews – 27 Mar 1879 (Marriage, **St. Thomas Parish**)

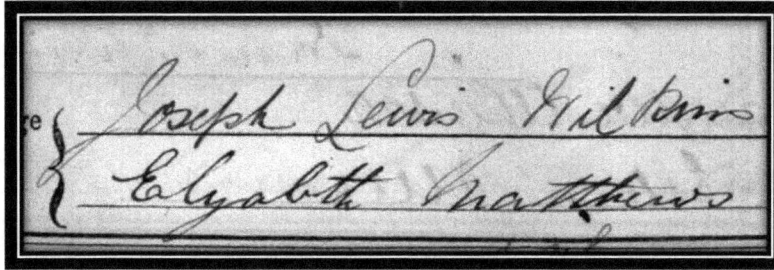

Signatures:

Joseph Lewis Wilkins (son):

Residence - 42 Upper Gloucester Street - March 27, 1879

Occupation - Compositor - March 27, 1879

Elizabeth Matthews, daughter of Michael Matthews (daughter-in-law):

Residence - 42 Upper Gloucester Street - March 27, 1879

Relationship Status at Marriage - minor age

Michael Matthews (father):

Occupation - Goldier

John Wilkins (father):

Occupation - Shop Keeper

Wedding Witnesses:

George William Tucker & Mary King

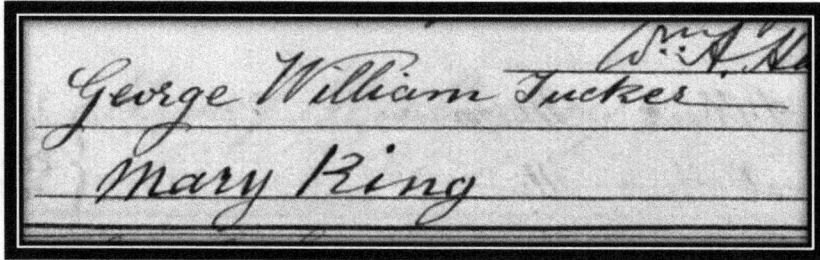

Signatures:

- Joseph Wilkins & Mary Wilkins

  - Charles Thomas Wilkins – b. 10 Feb 1877, bapt. 11 Nov 1877 (Baptism, **Rotunda Chapel Parish**)

Joseph Wilkins (father):

Residence - Beverley, Lancashire, England - November 11, 1877

Occupation - Servant - November 11, 1877

- Joshua Wilkins & Elizabeth Wilkins

  - Penelope Wilkins – bapt. 30 Oct 1704 (Baptism, **St. Mary Parish**)

  - Augustine Wilkins – bapt. 19 Jan 1706 (Baptism, **St. Mary Parish**)

Joshua Wilkins (father):

Occupation - Gentleman - October 30, 1704

January 19, 1706

- Matthew Wilkins & Margaret Wilkins

  - John Wilkins – bapt. 11 Jan 1778 (Baptism, **St. Mary Parish**)

Wilkins Surname Ireland: 1600s to 1900s

- Robert Wilkins & Elizabeth Wilkins

  o Henry Wilkins – bapt. 20 Jan 1862 (Baptism, **Arbour Hill Barracks Parish**)

Robert Wilkins (father):

Residence - Royal Barracks - January 20, 1862

Occupation - Servant to Lieutenant Colonel Henry O'Fielding, 2ⁿᵈ Guards

- Robert Wilkins & Mary Wilkins

  o Anne Wilkins – bapt. 27 Jun 1773 (Baptism, **Carlow Parish**)

- Robert Wilkins & Mary Anne Wilkins

  o William David Wilkins, b. 15 May 1851, bapt. 11 Jan 1852 (Baptism, **St. Peter Parish**) & Mary Jane Cameron – 14 Oct 1874 (Marriage, **St. Catherine Parish**)

Signatures:

- Mary Catherine Wilkins – b. 29 Oct 1874, bapt. 27 Dec 1874 (Baptism, **St. Werburgh Parish**)

- William Robert Wilkins – b. 15 May 1876, bapt. 1 Oct 1876 (Baptism, **St. Werburgh Parish**)

- Thomas Wilkins – b. 23 Oct 1877, bapt. 3 Feb 1878 (Baptism, **Molyneux Chapel Parish**)

- Frances Elizabeth Wilkins – b. 3 Jan 1880, bapt. 7 Mar 1880 (Baptism, **St. Werburgh Parish**)

- Albert Edward Wilkins – b. 4 Jul 1882, bapt. 10 Sep 1882 (Baptism, **St. Werburgh Parish**)

- William Robert Wilkins – b. 4 Sep 1884, bapt. 17 Mar 1885 (Baptism, **St. Peter Parish**)

- Arthur Wilkins – b. 10 May 1890, bapt. 4 Oct 1890 (Baptism, **St. Peter Parish**)

Hurst

William David Wilkins (son):

Residence - 6 Bride Street - October 14, 1874

December 27, 1874

October 1, 1876

4 Aungier Street - February 3, 1878

33 Castle Street - March 7, 1880

9 Aungier Street - September 10, 1882

70 Aungier Street - March 17, 1885

25 Aungier Street - October 4, 1890

Occupation - Upholsterer - October 14, 1874

December 27, 1874

October 1, 1876

February 3, 1878

March 7, 1880

September 10, 1882

March 17, 1885

October 4, 1890

Mary Jane Cameron, daughter of William Cameron (daughter-in-law):

Residence - 99 Cork Street - October 14, 1874

Wilkins Surname Ireland: 1600s to 1900s

William Cameron (father):

   Occupation - Commercial Clerk

Robert Wilkins (father):

   Occupation - Farmer

Wedding Witnesses:

Robert James Wilkins & Frances Jane Grattan

Signatures:

o   Robert James Wilkins & Frances Jane Grattan – 25 Apr 1875 (Marriage, **St. Catherine Parish**)

Signatures:

Signatures (Marriage):

Hurst

- Robert James Wilkins – b. 14 Jul 1876, bapt. 13 Aug 1876 (Baptism, **Molyneux Chapel Parish**)

- Margaret Jane Wilkins – b. 9 Oct 1878, bapt. 1 Dec 1878 (Baptism, **Molyneux Chapel Parish**)

- Frances Elizabeth Wilkins – b. 5 Sep 1880, bapt. 3 Nov 1880 (Baptism, **Leeson Park Parish**)

- Anne Florence Wilkins – b. 12 Aug 1882, bapt. 8 Oct 1882 (Baptism, **Leeson Park Parish**)

- Victoria Julia Ellen Wilkins – b. 6 Jun 1887, bapt. 21 Aug 1887 (Baptism, **Leeson Park Parish**)

Robert James Wilkins (son):

Residence - 6 Bride Street - April 25, 1875

16 Lower Mount Pleasant Avenue - August 13, 1876

December 1, 1878

November 3, 1880

October 8, 1882

13 Armstrong Street, Harold's Cross - August 21, 1887

Occupation - Cabinet Maker - April 25, 1875

August 13, 1876

December 1, 1878

November 3, 1880

October 8, 1882

August 21, 1887

Frances Jane Grattan, daughter of Robert Grattan (daughter-in-law):

Residence - 99 Cork Street - April 25, 1875

Robert Grattan (father):

    Occupation - Cord Cutter

Robert Wilkins (father):

    Occupation - Farmer

Wedding Witnesses:

Margaret Curtis & Samuel Grattan

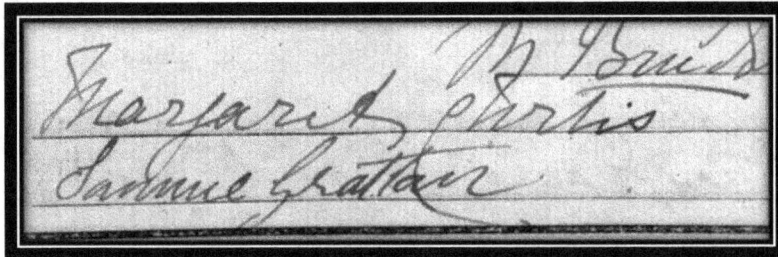

Signatures:

Robert Wilkins (father):

    Residence - No. 9 York Street - January 11, 1852

    Occupation - Porter - January 11, 1852

- Samuel Wilkins & Mary Anne Garrard – 10 Jun 1738 (Marriage, **St. Michan Parish**)

Samuel Wilkins (husband):

    Occupation - Gentleman - June 10, 1738

Mary Anne Garrard (wife):

    Occupation - Spinster - June 10, 1738

Hurst

- Thomas Wilkins & Alice Sarah Carrage – 20 Apr 1770 (Marriage, **St. Peter Parish**)

- Thomas Wilkins & Anne Hackett – 25 Jul 1791 (Marriage, **St. Nicholas Without Parish**)

- Thomas Wilkins & Catherine Scanlon – 7 Jul 1825 (Marriage, **St. James Parish**)

Thomas Wilkins (husband):

    Residence - St. James Parish - July 7, 1825

    Occupation - 22nd Regiment - July 7, 1825

Catherine Scanlon (wife):

    Residence - St. James Parish - July 7, 1825

Wedding Witnesses:

William Sparling & Francis Harvey

- Thomas Wilkins & Esther Hopkins – 25 Jun 1750 (Marriage, **St. Mark Parish**)

- Thomas Henry Wilkins & Sophie Emma Wilkins

  o Loftus Ralph Wilkins – b. 11 May 1854, bapt. 2 May 1856 (Baptism, **St. Peter Parish**)

  o Walter George Wilkins & Sophie Henrietta Nesbitt Barrett – 29 Feb 1872 (Marriage, **St. Stephen Parish**)

Signatures:

Wilkins Surname Ireland: 1600s to 1900s

Walter George Wilkins (son):

    Residence - 88 Leinster Road - February 29, 1872

    Occupation - Medical Doctor - February 29, 1872

Sophie Henrietta Nesbitt Barrett, daughter of William Barrett (daughter-in-law):

    Residence - 39 Lower Mount Street - February 29, 1872

William Barrett (father):

    Occupation - Soldier

Thomas Henry Wilkins (father):

    Occupation - Surgeon

Wedding Witnesses:

Anne Jules & W. Shaw

Signatures:

Thomas Henry Wilkins (father):

    Residence - Mountain View, Harold's Cross - May 2, 1856

    Occupation - Surgeon - May 2, 1856

- Unknown Wilkins & Unknown

  o John Wilkins

Signature:

- Unknown Wilkins & Unknown

  o Unknown Wilkins, d. bef. 21 Jul 1796 & Margaret Unknown (1st Marriage)

  o Margaret Unknown Wilkins (2nd Marriage) & Charles Leake – 21 Jul 1796 (Marriage, **St. Mary Parish**)

Margaret Unknown Wilkins (wife):

Relationship Status at 2nd Marriage - widow

- Unknown Wilkins & Unknown

  o Unknown Wilkins, d. bef. 20 Apr 1852 & Catherine Underwood (1st Marriage)

  o Catherine Underwood Wilkins (2nd Marriage) & William Metcalf – 20 Apr 1852 (Marriage, **St. Bride Parish**)

Signatures:

Wilkins Surname Ireland: 1600s to 1900s

Catherine Underwood Wilkins, daughter of James Underwood (wife):

    Residence - Harold's Cross - April 20, 1852

    Relationship Status at 2nd Marriage - widow

William Metcalf, son of Richard Metcalf (husband):

    Residence - South George's Street - April 20, 1852

    Occupation - Tobacconist - April 20, 1852

    Relationship Status at Marriage - widow

Richard Metcalf (father):

    Occupation - Farmer

James Underwood (father):

    Occupation - Gentleman

Wedding Witnesses:

Henry Barry D'Arcy & James Evans

Signatures:

Hurst

- William Wilkins & Elizabeth Bradley – 3 Nov 1811 (Marriage, **St. Andrew Parish**)

  - Sophie Wilkins – bapt. 28 Mar 1813 (Baptism, **St. Mary Parish**)

  - Anne Wilkins – b. 24 May 1814, bapt. 12 Jun 1814 (Baptism, **St. Mary Parish**)

  - Elizabeth Wilkins – bapt. 14 Jun 1816 (Baptism, **St. Mary Parish**)

  - John James Wilkins – b. 28 Jun 1821, bapt. 30 Jun 1821 (Baptism, **St. Mary Parish**)

  - William Bradley Wilkins – b. 28 Jun 1821, bapt. 30 Jun 1821 (Baptism, **St. Mary Parish**)

- William Wilkins & Elizabeth Wilkins

  - Maude Mary Wilkins – b. 8 Mar 1887, bapt. 1 Apr 1887 (Baptism, **Portobello Barracks Parish**)

William Wilkins (father):

Residence - Portobello Barracks - April 1, 1887

Occupation - B & R A [Royal Artillery] **- April 1, 1887**

- William Wilkins & Margaret Unknown

  - Catherine Wilkins – b. 1 Mar 1792, bapt. 9 Mar 1792 (Baptism, **St. Nicholas Without Parish**)

William Wilkins (father):

Residence - Patrick Street - March 9, 1792

- William Wilkins & Martha Unknown, b. 1740, bur. 2 Aug 1770 (Burial, **St. Werburgh Parish**)

  - James Wilkins – bapt. 1 Aug 1770 (Baptism, **St. Werburgh Parish**)

William Wilkins (father):

Residence - Dublin Castle - August 1, 1770

Wilkins Surname Ireland: 1600s to 1900s

Martha Unknown (mother):

Residence - Dublin Castle - before August 2, 1770

Age at Death - 30 years

Cause of Death - child birth

- William Wilkins & Mary Unknown
  - Elizabeth Wilkins – bapt. 10 Nov 1776 (Baptism, **St. Nicholas Without Parish**)
- William Wilkins & Mary Wilkins
  - Maurice Arthur Charles Wilkins – b. 8 Sep 1885, bapt. 24 Dec 1885 (Baptism, **St. Peter Parish**)
  - Edgar Henry Wilkins – b. 5 Sep 1887, bapt. 27 Dec 1887 (Baptism, **St. Peter Parish**)
  - Beatrice Una Wilkins – b. 28 Dec 1890, bapt. 12 Apr 1891 (Baptism, **St. Peter Parish**)
  - Lucy Mab Wilkins – b. 14 Feb 1895, bapt. 26 May 1895 (Baptism, **St. Peter Parish**)

William Wilkins (father):

Residence - 40 Harcourt Street - December 24, 1885

April 12, 1891

May 26, 1895

High School, Harcourt Street - December 27, 1887

Occupation - School Master - December 24, 1885

May 26, 1895

Head Master, High School - December 27, 1887

April 12, 1891

- William Wilkins & Sarah Nolan

  o Henry Wilkins – bapt. 8 Feb 1835 (Baptism, **Tralee Parish**), bapt. 28 Feb 1835 (Baptism, **Tralee Parish (RC)**)

William Wilkins (father):

Residence - Tralee Barracks - February 8, 1835

Occupation - Private, 37th Regiment - February 8, 1835

- William Wilkins & Unknown

  o Unknown Wilkins (Male Child) – bur. 15 Jan 1676 (Burial, **St. John Parish**)

  o Charles Wilkins – bapt. 20 Mar 1680 (Baptism, **St. John Parish**)

  o Fewphin Wilkins (Daughter) – bapt. 19 Jun 1681 (Baptism, **St. John Parish**)

- William Mortimer Wilkins & Sarah Wilkins

  o Mary Wilkins & Joseph Watkins – 7 Oct 1869 (Marriage, **St. Peter Parish**)

Signatures:

Wilkins Surname Ireland: 1600s to 1900s

Mary Wilkins (daughter):

   Residence - 18 Lower Mount Pleasant Avenue - October 7, 1869

   Relationship Status at Marriage - minor

Joseph Watkins, son of Joseph Watkins (son-in-law):

   Residence - 49 Belgreen Square, Rathmines - October 7, 1869

   Occupation - Esquire - October 7, 1869

Joseph Watkins (father):

   Occupation - Farmer

William Mortimer Wilkins (father):

   Occupation - Medical Doctor

Wedding Witnesses:

George Humphreys & Charles Henry Brien

Signatures:

- o   Elizabeth Wilkins – b. 4 Jul 1854, bapt. 19 Jul 1854 (Baptism, **St. George Parish**)

- o   Charles James Wilkins – b. 6 Jan 1856, bapt. 8 Feb 1856 (Baptism, **St. Peter Parish**)

- o   George Wilkins – b. 27 Jul 1858, bapt. 13 Aug 1858 (Baptism, **St. Peter Parish**)

Hurst

William Mortimer Wilkins (father):

Residence - 1 Madras Place - July 19, 1854

Harold's Cross - February 8, 1856

10 Harold's Cross - August 13, 1858

Occupation - Surgeon on Half Pay, 41st Regiment Foot - July 19, 1854

Surgeon - February 8, 1856

August 13, 1858

Individual Baptisms/Births

None Were Listed

Individual Burials

- Adeline Wilkins – b. 1847, bur. 4 Mar 1857 (Burial, **St. Mark Parish**)

Adeline Wilkins (deceased):

    Residence - 74 Harold's Cross - before March 4, 1857

    Age at Death - 10 years

    Cause of Death - water on the brain

- Anne Wilkins – b. 1777, bur. 3 Feb 1863 (Burial, **St. Mark Parish**)

Anne Wilkins (deceased):

    Residence - Mercer Street - before March 4, 1857

    Age at Death - 86 years

    Cause of Death - decay of nature

- Catherine Wilkins – b. 1751, bur. 18 Sep 1818 (Burial, **St. Peter Parish**)

Catherine Wilkins (deceased):

    Residence - Mount Lean's Lane - before September 18, 1818

    Age at Death - 67 years

Wilkins Surname Ireland: 1600s to 1900s

- Charles Wilkins – b. 1787, bur. 29 Jul 1842 (Burial, **St. Nicholas Without Parish**)

Charles Wilkins (deceased):

    Residence - Abbey Street - before July 29, 1842

    Age at Death - 55 years

- Henry Wilkins – bur. 13 Jan 1808 (Burial, **St. Paul Parish**)
- Henry Wilkins – bur. 22 Feb 1825 (Burial, **St. Nicholas Without Parish**)

Henry Wilkins (deceased):

    Residence - Abbey Street - before February 22, 1825

- Henry Wilkins – b. 1811, bur. 10 Feb 1858 (Burial, **St. George Parish**)

Henry Wilkins (deceased):

    Residence - St. George's Place - before February 10, 1858

    Age at Death - 47 years

- Henry Wilkins – bur. 9 Apr 1858 (Burial, **St. George Parish**)

Henry Wilkins (deceased):

    Residence - Old Men's Asylum - before April 9, 1858

- James Wilkins – bur. 23 Sep 1790 (Burial, **St. Paul Parish**)
- James Wilkins – bur. 20 Jan 1809 (Burial, **St. Paul Parish**)

Hurst

- Jane Wilkins – bur. 21 May 1826 (Burial, **St. James Parish**)

Jane Wilkins (deceased):

  Residence - Granville Lane - before May 21, 1826

- Jane Wilkins – b. 1830, bur. 21 Dec 1847 (Burial, **St. Matthew Parish**)

Jane Wilkins (deceased):

  Residence - Summer Hill, Dublin - before December 21, 1847

  Age at Death - 17 years

- John Wilkins – bur. 17 Apr 1749 (Burial, **St. Paul Parish**)

John Wilkins (deceased):

  Relationship Status at Death - single

- John Wilkins – bur. 11 Jan 1800 (Burial, **Glasnevin Parish**)

John Wilkins (deceased):

  Residence - Crow Street - before January 11, 1800

- John Wilkins – bur. 13 Apr 1809 (Burial, **St. Paul Parish**)
- John Wilkins – bur. 17 Oct 1813 (Burial, **St. Catherine Parish**)

John Wilkins (deceased):

  Residence - Cork Street - before October 17, 1813

Wilkins Surname Ireland: 1600s to 1900s

- John Wilkins – b. 1776, bur. 5 Feb 1859 (Burial, **St. Mark Parish**)

John Wilkins (deceased):

    Residence - 27 Camden Street - before February 5, 1859

    Age at Death - 83 years

    Cause of Death - asthma

- Matthew Wilkins – b. 1800, bur. 9 Sep 1822 (Burial, **St. Mary Parish**)

Matthew Wilkins (deceased):

    Residence - Stafford Street - before September 9, 1822

    Age at Death - 22 years

- Mary Wilkins – bur. 24 Jul 1745 (Burial, **St. Paul Parish**)
- Mary Wilkins – b. 1775, bur. 30 Mar 1855 (Burial, **St. Paul Parish**)

Mary Wilkins (deceased):

    Residence - Irishtown - before March 30, 1855

    Age at Death - 80 years

- Mary Catherine Wilkins – b. 1756, bur. 23 Mar 1828 (Burial, **St. Mary Parish**)

Mary Catherine Wilkins (deceased):

    Residence - Abbey Street - before March 23, 1828

    Age at Death - 72 years

- Rebecca Wilkins – bur. 9 Oct 1803 (Burial, **Glasnevin Parish**)

Rebecca Wilkins (deceased):

Residence - Bolton Street - before October 9, 1803

- Samuel Wilkins – bur. 3 Sep 1844 (Burial, **St. Matthew Parish**)

Samuel Wilkins (deceased):

Residence - Irishtown - before September 3, 1844

- Sarah Wilkins – bur. 16 Sep 1735 (Burial, **St. Paul Parish**)

Sarah Wilkins (deceased):

Age at Death - child

- Singleton Wilkins – bur. 9 May 1832 (Burial, **Carlow Parish**)

Singleton Wilkins (deceased):

Occupation - Esquire - before May 9, 1832

- Stephen Wilkins – bur. 17 Oct 1819 (Burial, **St. James Parish**)

Stephen Wilkins (deceased):

Residence - Dorset Street - before October 17, 1819

- Susan Wilkins – b. 1772, bur. 3 Apr 1856 (Burial, **St. Catherine Parish**)

Susan Wilkins (deceased):

Residence - Parochial Widow House, Marrowbone Lane - April 3, 1856

Age at Death - 84 years

Wilkins Surname Ireland: 1600s to 1900s

- Thomas Wilkins – bur. 13 Jun 1785 (Burial, **St. James Parish**)

Thomas Wilkins (deceased):

    Residence - Cork Street - before June 13, 1785

- Thomas Henry Wilkins – b. 1802, bur. 6 Jul 1885 (Burial, **St. Mark Parish**)

Thomas Henry Wilkins (deceased):

    Residence - 88 Leinster Road - before July 6, 1885

    Occupation - Surgeon - before July 6, 1885

    Age at Death - 83 years

- Unknown Wilkins – bur. 22 Mar 1756 (Burial, **St. Nicholas Without Parish**)
- Unknown Wilkins – bur. 17 Jul 1778 (Burial, **St. Nicholas Within Parish**) (Burial, **St. Nicholas Without Parish**)

Unknown Wilkins (deceased):

    Residence - Patrick Street - before July 17, 1778

- Unknown Wilkins – bur. 6 Oct 1779 (Burial, **St. Nicholas Without Parish**)

Unknown Wilkins (deceased):

    Residence - Patrick Street - before October 6, 1779

- Unknown Wilkins – bur. 8 Nov 1784 (Burial, **St. Nicholas Without Parish**)

Unknown Wilkins (deceased):

    Residence - George's Street - before November 8, 1784

Hurst

- Unknown Wilkins – bur. 1 Oct 1787 (Burial, **St. Nicholas Without Parish**)

Unknown Wilkins (deceased):

  Residence - Patrick Street - before October 1, 1787

- Unknown Wilkins – bur. 13 Jul 1788 (Burial, **St. Nicholas Without Parish**)

Unknown Wilkins (deceased):

  Residence - Patrick Street - before July 13, 1788

- Unknown Wilkins – bur. 9 Dec 1789 (Burial, **St. Nicholas Without Parish**)

Unknown Wilkins (deceased):

  Residence - Patrick Street - before December 9, 1789

- Unknown Wilkins (Mr.) – bur. 22 Sep 1793 (Burial, **St. Mary Parish**)

Unknown Wilkins (Mr.) (deceased):

  Residence - Abbey Street - before September 22, 1793

- Unknown Wilkins (Mr.) – bur. 5 Sep 1810 (Burial, **St. Mary Parish**)

Unknown Wilkins (Mr.) (deceased):

  Residence - Abbey Street - before September 5, 1810

- Unknown Wilkins (Mr.) – b. 1785, bur. 2 Oct 1831 (Burial, **St. Mary Parish**)

Unknown Wilkins (Mr.) (deceased):

  Residence - Abbey Street - before October 2, 1831

  Age at Death - 46 years

Wilkins Surname Ireland: 1600s to 1900s

- William Wilkins – bur. 6 Jan 1682 (Burial, **St. Audoen Parish**)

- William Wilkins – bur. 26 Jul 1811 (Burial, **St. Paul Parish**)

- William Wilkins – b. 1823, bur. 9 Mar 1830 (Burial, **St. Peter Parish**)

William Wilkins (deceased):

    Residence - Camden Street - before March 9, 1830

    Age at Death - 7 years

- William Wilkins – d. 22 Mar 1836, bur. 1836 (Burial, **St. James Parish**)

William Wilkins (deceased):

    Residence - Donnybrook - March 22, 1836

- William Wilkins – b. 1824, bur. 23 Jan 1844 (Burial, **St. Paul Parish**)

William Wilkins (deceased):

    Residence - Royal Infirmary - before January 23, 1844

    Occupation - Private, 1st Royals - before January 23, 1844

    Age at Death - 20 years

- William Wilkins – b. 1806, bur. 12 Dec 1846 (Burial, **St. Peter Parish**)

William Wilkins (deceased):

    Residence - Lacy's Lane - before December 12, 1846

    Age at Death - 40 years

Individual Marriages

- Anne Wilkins & Barnabas (B a r n a b a s) Russell – 16 Nov 1727 (Marriage, **St. Peter Parish**)

Barnabas Russell (husband):

Residence - Consistory Court - November 16, 1727

- Anne Wilkins & John Hughes – 12 Jul 1817 (Marriage, **St. Andrew Parish (RC)**)

Wedding Witnesses:

Michael Keller & Jane Dunne

- Arabella Wilkins & William Sleater – 24 Sep 1822 (Marriage, **St. Peter Parish**)

Arabella Wilkins (wife):

Residence - St. Peter Parish - September 24, 1822

William Sleater (husband):

Residence - St. Peter Parish - September 24, 1822

Wedding Witnesses:

P. W. Mile & Robert Mills

- Catherine Wilkins & Joseph Gilmore – 13 Oct 1828 (Marriage, **St. Andrew Parish (RC)**)

Wedding Witnesses:

Margaret Ryan & Matthew Murphy

Wilkins Surname Ireland: 1600s to 1900s

- Elizabeth Wilkins & Daniel McDaniel – 22 Nov 1763 (Marriage, **St. Werburgh Parish**)

- Elizabeth Wilkins & Edward Hamilton

  o   Anne Hamilton – bapt. 11 Feb 1849 (Baptism, **Rathmines Parish (RC)**)

- Elizabeth Wilkins & John Proctor – 5 Feb 1772 (Marriage, **Carlow Parish**)

- Elizabeth Wilkins & Samuel Hattanvil – 9 Apr 1730 (Marriage, **St. Mary Parish**)

- Esther Wilkins & James Terry – 16 Jun 1755 (Marriage, **St. Mark Parish**)

- Jane Wilkins & James Burges – 11 Aug 1812 (Marriage, **Chapelizod Parish**)

James Burges (husband):

Residence - Private in Army - August 11, 1812

- Mary Wilkins & Hugh Murphy

  o   Mary Murphy – b. 6 Feb 1857, bapt. 5 Apr 1858 (Baptism, **St. James Parish (RC)**)

Hugh Murphy (father):

Residence - Island Bridge - April 5, 1858

- Mary Wilkins & James Malone

  o   James John Malone – bapt. 29 Dec 1850 (Baptism, **St. Nicholas Parish (RC)**)

- Mary Wilkins & James Price

  o   James Joseph Price – b. 1876, bapt. 1898 (Baptism, **Lucan Parish (RC)**)

James Price (father):

Residence - Blackpool, England - 1898

Hurst

- Mary Wilkins & John Hunter

  o Charles Hunter & Susan Guthrie – 13 Dec 1893 (Marriage, **St. Mary, Pro Cathedral Parish (RC)**)

Charles Hunter (son):

Residence - 2 Sackville Avenue - December 13, 1893

Susan Guthrie, daughter of Philip Guthrie & Dora Carey (daughter-in-law):

Residence - 29 Lower Rutland Street - December 13, 1893

Wedding Witnesses:

Michael Molphy & Ellen Molphy

- Mary Wilkins & Peter O'Brien

  o Elizabeth O'Brien – b. 1862, bapt. 1862 (Baptism, **St. Andrew Parish (RC)**)

Peter O'Brien (father):

Residence - 28 King Street - 1862

- Rosetta Wilkins & John Thomas Doyle

  o Christopher John Angel Doyle – b. 26 Jul 1863, bapt. 29 Aug 1863 (Baptism, **Rathmines Parish (RC)**)

  o James T. Doyle – b. 18 Mar 1867, bapt. 9 Apr 1867 (Baptism, **Rathmines Parish (RC)**)

John Thomas Doyle (father):

Residence - London - August 29, 1863

Belgrave Square - April 9, 1867

Wilkins Surname Ireland: 1600s to 1900s

- Sarah Wilkins & Thomas Carroll

  o Thomas Carroll – bapt. 24 Sep 1848 (Baptism, **St. James Parish (RC)**)

Name Variations

Includes Latin and Abbreviated forms of names found in the original documents.

Abigail = Abigale, Abigall

Anne = Ann, Anna, Annae

Bartholomew = Barth, Bartholmeus, Bartholomeo

Bridget = Birgis, Brigid, Brigida, Bridgit

Catherine = Catharine, Catharina, Catharinae, Catherina, Cath, Catha, Cathae, Cathe, Cathn, Kate

Charles = Carolus, Charls, Chas

Christopher = Christoph

Daniel = Danielem, Danielis

Edmund = Edmond

Edward = Ed, Edwd

Eleanor = Eleo, Eleonora, Elinor, Ellenor

Elizabeth = Betty, Elisa, Elisabeth, Eliz, Eliza, Elizab, Elizh, Elizth

Ellen = Elena, Ellena

Emily = Emilia

Esther = Essie, Ester

Francis = Fransicum

George = Geo, Georg, Georgius

Grace = Gratiae

Gulielmo = Guil, Guillelmi, Gulielmum, Guillelmus, Gulmi

Helen = Helena

Wilkins Surname Ireland: 1600s to 1900s

Honor = Hanora, Honora

James = Jacobi, Jacobus, Jas

Jane = Joanna

Jeanne = Jeannae, Joannae

Joan = Johanna, Joney

John = Jno, Joannem, Joannes, Johannis

Joseph = Jos

Juliana = Julian

Leticia = Letitia, Lettice, Letticia

Lewis = Louis

Luke = Lucas

Margaret = Margarita, Margaritae, Margeret, Marget, Margt

Martha = Marthae

Mary = Maria, My

Mary Anne = Marianna, Marianne, Maryanne

Michael = Michaelis, Michl

Patrick = Pat, Patt, Patk, Patricii, Patricius

Peter = Petri

Richard = Ricardi, Ricardus, Rich, Richd

Robert = Roberti

Rose = Rosa, Rosae

Thomas = Thom, Thomae, Thoms, Thos, Ths

Timothy = Timotheus, Timy

William = Wil, Will, Willm, Wm

Notes

Notes

Notes

Notes

Notes

Notes

Index

T

U

Hurst

George Lewis
1813 Sep 5 14

Harriet
1818 Jul 10 12

Helen Honor
1850 Apr 2 13

Henry
1813 Aug 23 12
1835 Feb 8 30
1862 Jan 20 19

Henry Cornwall Christopher
1876 Jan 12 6

James
1770 Aug 1 28

Jeremiah
1789 Nov 22 9

John
1778 Jan 11 18
1785 Mar 22 9
1842 Jun 12 8
1842 Jun 5 8

John James
1821 Jun 30 28

Joseph
1786 Jun 7 9

Loftus Ralph
1856 May 2 24

Lucy
1806 Feb 5 12

Lucy Mab
1895 May 26 29

Margaret
1806 Feb 5 12
1814 Jul 31 7

Margaret Jane
1878 Dec 1 22

Martha
1779 Aug 22 5

Mary
1841 Jan 18 4

Mary Anne
1792 Jan 27 5
1865 Feb 20 7

Mary Catherine

1874 Dec 27 19

Maude Mary
1887 Apr 1 28

Maurice Arthur Charles
1885 Dec 24 29

Penelope
1704 Oct 30 18

Robert
1737 Oct 24 13

Robert James
1876 Aug 13 22

Samuel
1761 Oct 21 13

Sophie
1813 Mar 28 28

Thomas
1878 Feb 3 19

Thomas Henry
1838 7

Victoria Julia Ellen
1887 Aug 21 22

William
1784 Jun 27 5
1790 9
1795 Nov 8 5

William Bradley
1821 Jun 30 28

William David
1852 Jan 11 19

William Robert
1876 Oct 1 19
1885 Mar 17 19

Births

Adeline
1847 34

Albert Edward
1882 Jul 4 19

Alfred Thomas
1879 May 18 13

Anne
1777 34
1814 May 24 28

Anne Florence
1882 Aug 12 22

Wilkins Surname Ireland: 1600s to 1900s

Wilkins Surname Ireland: 1600s to 1900s

About The Author

Donovan Hurst graduated from San Diego State University with a Bachelor of Arts in the major field of studies of History and a minor in the field of studies of Anthropology. He is a current member of The General Society of Mayflower Descendants and has been conducting genealogical research for over 10 years tracing back his ancestors to their ancestral homelands in Denmark, England, France, Germany, Ireland, Norway, and Scotland.

www.ingramcontent.com/pod-product-compliance
Lightning Source LLC
Chambersburg PA
CBHW081200270326
41930CB00014B/3240